MARTYR HAMID RAHIMAIAN

STORY OF A MARTYR

IMRAN KASHMIRI

Made with ♥ on the Notion Press Platform
www.notionpress.com

Dr. Hamed Rahimian
Assistant Professor

Department of Industrial Engineering
277C Freeman Hall, Clemson University
Clemson, SC 29634-0920 Ph.D. Industrial and Systems
Engineering, The Ohio State University, 2018
Major: Operations Research, Minors: Mathematics and
Statistics
M.S. Industrial Engineering, Sharif University of
Technology, Tehran, Iran, 2011
B.S. Industrial Engineering, Sharif University of
Technology, Tehran, Iran, 2008
Professional Affiliations

Member, Institute of Industrial and Systems Engineers
(IISE)
Member, Institute for Operations Research and the
Management Sciences (INFORMS)
Member, Society of Industrial and Applied Mathematics
(SIAM)
Member, Mathematical Optimization Society (MOS)
Member, American Society of Civil Engineers (ASCE),
Environmental & Water Resources Institute (EWRI

Contents

Foreword

The distinctive characteristic of a martyr is that he charges the atmosphere with courage and zeal. He revives the spirit of valor and fortitude ... among the people who have lost it. That is why Islam is always in need of martyrs.

When Imam Hosein decided to leave for Kufa, some prudent members of his family tried to dissuade him. Their argument was that his action was not logical. They were right in their own way. ... But Imam Hosein had a higher logic. His logic was that of a martyr, which is beyond the comprehension of ordinary people.

Preface

As Hamid's story unfolded, his body seized up as he stuttered and choked out the words. His pale face twisted in pain. "I was in a truck with twenty-one others," he said with difficulty. "We were on the road between Khorramshahr and Ahwaz. The Iraqis surrounded us with tanks. One tank hit us hard. Five of my comrades were martyred immediately. Cut into pieces. The rest of us were badly injured."

Hamid's lungs were seared and permanently scarred. His heart was damaged. Both arms and legs were badly broken. The cruel irony is that the attack came on September 9, 1988, after Iran and Iraq had signed a cease-fire ending their eight-year war. "These are my last days," Hamid told me more than a decade later. "The doctors don't have hope anymore. I know that I will die soon. That is when I'll begin my new life."

Every day for five years he has come to his office in the House of Martyrs in the center of Behesht-e Zahra, Tehran's vast cemetery, to fall under death's spell. The job pays the equivalent of $45 a month. Still, Hamid feels privileged. "I came here to work because my friends are buried here," he said. "They told me that if they died I must follow their path. The Koran says, 'Those who die for God are martyrs, and the martyrs never die. They live forever.'"

Hamid is a Shiite, and he fervently believes in the Shiite version of history, its lore and its rituals. Ayatollah Khomeini had told the Hamids of Iran that martyrdom was a perfect death, and they believed him. If they couldn't die, at least they could keep that spirit alive.

For Shiites, the battle of Karbala is the equivalent of the passion and crucifixion of Jesus, the self-flagellation reminiscent of the medieval practice of self-mutilation, carrying of the Cross, and physical deprivation that survives in parts of the Christian world today. In recent years during Moharram, the month of mourning, Iran's authorities tried to ban the most excessive ritual in which worshippers shave their heads and carve them open with swords. As Ayatollah Khamenei said in denouncing the ritual in 1999, it "gives the impression that Shiite Muslims are superstitious and irrational."

Even so, the cult of martyrdom has deep roots in Iran's Shiite culture, and Khomeini was a master at manipulating the homegrown strain of martyrdom and its lust for sacrifice. During a sermon in Qom for Moharram in 1963 Khomeini likened the oppression of the Iranian people under the Shah's monarchy to Hosein's martyrdom. When Khomeini was arrested shortly afterward, men and women alike wrapped themselves in white funeral shrouds as symbols of their readiness to die for him.

Once the struggle for power was joined, the spilling of blood came to be embraced, not avoided. As Iran's revolution was unfolding during the Moharram ceremony in 1978, demonstrators caught in a battle with the Shah's troops smeared their hands with the blood of the victims and raised their palms toward heaven. In the months before the revolution Khomeini said, "Our movement is but a fragile plant. It needs the blood of martyrs to help it grow into a towering tree." The Black Friday Massacre in Tehran on September 8, 1978, in which hundreds of demonstrators were killed by the Shah's troops, was a key event in precipitating the downfall of the Shah. Khomeini called that day the "victory of blood over the sword."

When Khomeini returned to Iran in 1979 he had his priorities right, Hamid told me. The first thing Khomeini did was to fly by helicopter to this very cemetery to mourn the victims of Black Friday. He was hoisted onto a platform, where he raised a fist before tens of thousands of his followers. "For those of you who have given up so much for God, God must soon give you the prize," he told them.

But now, more than two decades later, Hamid was still waiting for the prize.

Hamid seemed to know every road, every monument, every grave in Behesht-e Zahra, even though it extended for miles over a vast plain off the busy highway leading out of Tehran to Qom. The cemetery had been built in the 1950s and had expanded over the years to become Tehran's principal burial ground. As one of the few public spaces in Tehran safe from attack by the security forces before the revolution, it became, in addition, a meeting place for opponents of the Shah.

Today, a sculpture of a great white hand holding a red tulip, the flower of martyrdom, beckons visitors at the entrance of the complex. Inside, men and women gather to lay wreaths, pour rosewater, and recite verses of the Koran as they caress the tombstones of their dead husbands in an effort to make contact with their spirits. The cemetery is well organized for visitors, with a playground, park benches, public toilets, a convenience store, a computer center for locating graves, a kebab restaurant and a planned Metro station.

A walk through Behesht-e Zahra is a walk through the Islamic Republic's political history. One section houses the bodies of the National Front leaders, Islamic liberal intellectuals who opposed the Shah and joined forces with Khomeini. A second section is reserved for the victims of the Shah's secret police and military during the revolution. A third is assigned to officials killed in the terrorist bombing of the headquarters of the revolution's Islamic Republic Party in 1981. The section where Hamid works houses acres of graves for the martyrs of the Iran-Iraq war.

From 1980 through 1988, when the country was at war with Iraq, the wide, tree-lined roads at Behesht-e Zahra seemed perpetually clogged with mourners. Professional flagellators-for-hire wandered about in those days, prepared with wooden-handled bunches of chains to whip across their backs and shoulders in frenzied rituals of mourning. Military musicians playing saxophones, clarinets, trumpets, and drums sometimes accompanied the caskets of particularly important martyrs. Visiting the cemetery became a form of recreation, with extended families picnicking on the graves amid the evergreens and junipers and along the canals as they watched the spectacles. Mullahs told stories about martyrdom -- for pay -- in singsong voices that made people cry.

On the day I met Hamid, the martyrs' section was nearly deserted. But that didn't diminish his enthusiasm. He led me through rows and rows of graves of small slabs of gray stone set into concrete. Marking each grave is a framed glass case containing both religious icons and intensely intimate mementos: Koranic texts, green banners bearing religious inscriptions, worry beads, and prayer stones, next to plastic childhood toys and figurines from wedding cakes. Some of the cases include bits of tattered and bloody clothing worn by the victims at the time of their deaths. But there is something else, startling to an American: photographs of the dead that stare back.

The war martyrs look so hopeful. And so young. The colored polyester flags that fly from the metal cases -- for the Islamic Republic, for Islam, for mourning, for martyrdom, for the army, for the ready-to-die volunteers -- add a macabre festive look. Hamid showed me the grave in plot twenty-six that he said sometimes gives off the smell of perfumed flowers, even though no flowers grow there. And the grave in plot twenty-seven where the spirit of Fatemeh, Mohammad's daughter, comes and cries out in the middle of the night. ("Behesht-e Zahra" means "Paradise of Zahra," one of the names given to Fatemeh.) And the grave in plot twenty-four where a mother of a martyr named Ali Derakhshani built a tiny house of green metal for herself years ago, enabling her to live above her son's grave. An empty grave nearby awaits the woman.

Hamid showed me another grave in plot twenty-four where Hosein Fahmideh, a thirteen-year-old suicide bomber, is buried. In 1981, the story goes, Fahmideh strapped a bomb to his belly, crawled under an Iraqi tank, and blew himself up. Khomeini later called the boy "our leader," adding, "The value of his little heart is greater than could be described by hundreds of tongues and hundreds of pens. ... He drank the sweet elixir of martyrdom." In 1986, Iran celebrated his martyrdom by issuing a commemorative stamp. The occasion was the annual Universal Day of the Child.

Hamid showed me the high, wide-tiered fountain built for the martyred war dead. The fountain had once cascaded crimson-colored water dyed to look like blood. As more war dead came home, the cemetery grew bigger, so big that satellite fountains of martyrs' blood had to be built. The martyrs are "irrigating the revolutionary seed," officials liked to say. But after the war, the fountains were turned off. On the day of my visit, the main one was dry. When I asked Hamid why, he shrugged and said, "There are many things that have lost their color after twenty years. One of them is the color of the fountain. Some traitorous officials claim that the red color is a reminder of the blood shed during the war and since there is no war the fountain should not run red anymore. If it were up to me, I would build fountains in every single square in the country and fill them with red water to remind people of the sacrifices of the martyrs." ...

Acknowledgements

BY FAR THE BEST WAY to keep the memories fresh, Hamid told me, is to watch war films in the cemetery's theater hall. On the day of my visit, we were the only people in the audience. The theater was stuffy, the films grainy and grisly. He chose one of his favorites. It was about the return of the remains of Iranian soldiers years after the war. In one scene, a widow is given the bones of her husband. She picks them up one by one and kisses them, smiling, as if in a trance. She caresses the skull and speaks to it. "Your baby child is a man now!" she cries.

In another film a group of teenage soldiers prepare for a battle. They strap on their weapons and fire artillery against the enemy. They run up hills and fire handheld weapons and machine guns from behind sandbags. Then they begin to die. In one scene, two soldiers drag the body of a wounded comrade who has lost both his legs. The camera focuses on the bloody stumps. In another, the camera zooms in on the body of a decapitated soldier propped up on sandbags. In a third, a body has been cut in two. In a fourth, a sixteen-year-old soldier with both legs sliced off screams in agony, "Allah! Allah! Allah! Allah! I die for you, Hosein! I give up my life for you!"

As we watched, Hamid wept so deeply that I wanted to reach out to console him. But I knew my touch would be rebuffed. "These are the scenes I have seen!" he moaned. "I can never come back to life. I feel martyrdom with my two hands!"

The only time Hamid smiled in the hours we spent together was when he showed me a three-minute black and white film of his unit preparing for their fateful operation the day their truck was hit. One shot showed a much younger Hamid looking shyly at the camera as he boarded a bus headed to the front.

"We gave up the best days of our lives," Hamid said. "We gave up our education. Some of us died. Some of us were wounded. Now the ideals we fought for have been buried. The new generation doesn't want us anymore. This country is becoming so materialistic. It is losing its martyrdom mentality. Even worse, there is a plot to eliminate the fighting generation."

Hamid cursed the authorities in Tehran for building cultural centers and high-rise apartment complexes instead of better graves for the martyrs and more museums in their honor.

He cursed society for forgetting the sacrifices of his generation, telling the story of how he once fell ill on the street, but was turned away from a hospital because he didn't have the money to pay.

He cursed the privileged sons of high-ranking officials who drove fancy cars and carried mobile phones and even socialized openly with young women.

He cursed commercial filmmakers for presenting sanitized versions of the war. "They show soldiers clean, their hair full of gel," he said. "It's humiliating. It makes a joke of what we endured."

He cursed the United States for the "crimes" it committed over decades -- in Vietnam, in Iran, in Nicaragua.

Nicaragua? I hadn't thought about Nicaragua in a long time. "What were America's crimes in Nicaragua?" I asked Hamid.

"I don't remember," he said. "But I know they were bad."

He also blamed the United States for Iraq's war with Iran. In that, at least, I found a refrain that was common among Iranians of all political leanings and all degrees of religious fervor: the United States and its Western partners wanted Saddam Hussein to go to war against Iran to keep their country weak and force its experiment with revolution to fail. Iranians found proof of that in the world's reaction to Saddam's invasion in 1980. The United States merely cautioned that it "could not condone" Iraq's seizure of Iran's province of Khuzestan. It took the United Nations Security Council more than a week to pass a resolution that urged the combatants "to refrain immediately from any further use of force." The resolution did not call for a cease-fire or for a withdrawal of Iraq's troops to its borders. And it did not threaten any military action against Iraq as it would ten years later after Iraq invaded Kuwait.

Though there is no evidence that the United States played a part in Iraq's invasion, the American tilt toward Iraq after Iran went on the offensive in 1982 and the coordination of a global arms embargo of Iran convinced Iranians that the United States had taken sides. Toward the end of the war, the United States shared intelligence with Iraq on Iranian troop strength, which the Iraqis used in their offensives. And as part of its protection of oil tankers in the Persian Gulf, the U.S. Navy sank Iran's ships, destroyed oil platforms, and captured and killed Iranian crew members. Hamid saw America's continued military presence in the Gulf as evidence of a strategy to dominate Iran.

Hamid's final curses were reserved for President Khatami, who, he felt, had abandoned the generation of the war. Khatami had not even come to visit the martyrs' graves to commemorate the twentieth anniversary of the revolution.

Khatami, in fact, was no believer in permanent sacrifice. He had even stopped groups from chanting "Death to America" during a speech he gave to tens of thousands of students at the University of Tehran in May 1998, on the first anniversary of his election as President. "In any gathering in which I am present," he said, "I would prefer there to be talk of life and not death." ...

[Ayatollah] Khamenei was Hamid's hero, a "war-disabled" himself, Hamid said, because of the injuries suffered in a 1981 assassination attempt. "The leader came here and prayed in the martyrs' section for an hour," Hamid said. "He thanked us. He told us to stay on the path of the martyrs. I kissed his hand."

"Is the country going on the wrong path, then?" I asked.

"One hundred percent," Hamid replied. Then he stopped himself. "This conversation may get too political." Hamid did not want me to see his reflection in the mirror too clearly. I knew that I had pushed far enough, and backed off.

Hamid acknowledged that he was fighting on a more mundane battlefield now, to keep his job as the cemetery hired new employees with different ideas. "The new ones are bureaucrats who just come to the office and sign papers," he complained. "They haven't seen their friends die in a sea of their own blood."

The grisly footage in the hot auditorium had made me sick to my stomach. I asked to be shown to the ladies' room. Hamid proudly showed me a sign that read, "This way to the American and Israeli embassies." That's what the toilets at the martyrs' museum are called.

"So show me to my embassy," I said.

"What do you mean?" he asked.

"The American embassy."

"You're American?" he asked in disbelief. "I didn't know. They said you were French. I'm so, so sorry."

With much fanfare, Hamid ordered a subordinate to take down the sign. Hamid tore it up in little bits as he led me down the stairs.

When I came back up to say goodbye, we talked about the war front again. I told him that I had covered the war as a reporter and had also seen the carnage, from both sides of the border, including the aftermath of a battle in which the Iraqis had used chemical weapons against the Iranians.

"What a tragedy that you could not have found martyrdom at the battlefield," he said.

"But I don't want to die," I protested. "My kids need me. And your son needs you too."

"I try not to love him too much, so that he will not miss me when I die," Hamid said of his two-year-old son, Mohammad.

"Well then, love him until you die," I said.

It was then that Hamid let down his guard. Proud like any father, he said, "Oh, sometimes I take him to the playground. He's a great kid. Maybe you can come to our house and meet him one day."

"Inshallah," I said, "God willing," knowing it would never happen.

Hamid then surprised me again. The man who hated and cursed America wanted to visit. "Maybe I can take some time off and learn English," he said. "Can you help me get a passport and a visa?"

I suddenly found myself connecting with Hamid. I had gotten him to admit he was proud of his son. Now he was talking about visiting the United States. "Would you come?" I asked incredulously.

"Yes," he replied.

"Would you really come?"

The significance of his confession finally sunk in.

"Uh, no, no," he said. "There's too much corruption there."

But perhaps Hamid wasn't quite ready to die.

Prologue

IRAN CAME OUT

of the war sobered, convinced of the futility of armed force as a means of settling its international conflicts. When an American-led coalition went to war against Iraq in 1991, Iran stayed out.

Keeping alive the spirit of martyrdom in the minds of the Iranian people became harder. "The major casualty of the war," wrote the Iranian-born historian and author Shahram Chubin in 1989, "has been the credibility of the Islamic Republic among its own rank and file. It will no longer be able to effectively call upon its populace for crusades and sacrifices, but will have to act more like a normal state." Some critics of the system even called for the abolition of the baseej volunteer corps. Within the next decade, Iran's economy was in such crisis that the government began to sell exemptions to the two years of compulsory military service. A complex sliding scale was created: a Ph.D. paid three times what a high school dropout did. Mehdi Mahdavi-Kia, a star on the national soccer team, was exempted from the draft as a reward for scoring a spectacular second-half goal in Iran's World Cup soccer victory over the United States in 1998.

To preserve what is left of the war mentality, pockets of resistance within the leadership, hard-core believers, continue to train a new generation of would-be martyrs. Every summer, hundreds of teenage boys and girls from all over the country are brought to the Bahonar Camping Center, a sprawling, beautifully landscaped estate in the mountains high above Tehran, for an all-expenses-paid week of prayers, revolutionary songs, and inspiration. Most of them are the sons and daughters of men who died in the war with Iraq.

On a recent visit, I attended a rally in a vast auditorium decorated with photos of Ayatollahs Khomeini and Khamenei. The boys sat in front, the red kerchiefs of the baseej around their necks. A young woman sitting next to me in the back showed me her spiral notebook. On the front, where an American teenager might tape a picture of a rock star, she had taped a photo of Khomeini.

A short, bearded middle-aged man in glasses whipped up the group's emotions. Holding up a photograph of an unnamed martyr, he shouted, "I saw the bullets hitting his face and his body and I wanted to throw myself into the war." He told the story of a young woman who scooped up soil from the battlefront. "The soil was bloody, bloody, bloody," he sobbed. "She put it into a flower bed to help the flowers grow." He told the stories with the same long laments used by the mullahs in the mosques to encourage the faithful to weep on special days of mourning, and each reminiscence drove him and his audience to weeping. One teenage girl uttered a piercing cry. She fainted and was carried from the hall. Even the boys were sobbing now.

Sometime after the visit, I asked Khatami's chef de cabinet, Mohammad-Ali Abtahi, about the baseej camp and what purpose it serves. "These are the same types of people who beat their chests at the mourning rituals," he said. "But we can't expect our youth to beat their chests and mourn every day. Even if they insist on doing this we shouldn't all follow it because it leads to extremism. Joy and happiness is a part of youth too."

"But these are government-funded camps," I replied. "Why not shut them down?" He answered with a shrug. Clearly this is a part of the Islamic Republic that the

President does not control. The camp represents a side of Iran that seems to have been made permanently sad and twisted, one that remains stuck in the grisly psychology of a cult of martyrdom.

Yet it is hard for me to believe this war fever can be sustained. That's because there are so many other pieces in the mosaic that is Iranian society, illustrating that flexibility and improvisation can bring renewal even after so dark a period of horror.

The word "martyrdom" is a manifestation of self-sacrifice, Leader of the Islamic Revolution Ayatollah Seyyed Ali Khamenei said, stressing that conveying the martyrs' message to the new generation is necessary.

The word "martyrdom" is a manifestation of self-sacrifice, Leader of the Islamic Revolution Ayatollah Seyyed Ali Khamenei said, stressing that conveying the martyrs' message to the new generation is necessary.

Addressing the organizers of the second National Congress for Martyrs of Qom Province, Leader of the Islamic Revolution Ayatollah Seyyed Ali Khamenei touched upon the prominent figures of martyrs who sacrificed their lives on the path of God.

With regard to martyrdom, the title "martyr" is a title that cannot be easily overlooked. The word "martyr" encompasses a set of religious, national, and human values. When you say "martyr," this word is actually a book in itself. A set of religious teachings are contained within this word. A set of national teachings are contained within this word. A set of moral teachings and virtues are contained within this word. It is a very important word, Ayatollah Khamenei said in this meeting.

The word martyr is a collection of religious, national, and moral teachings. As for religious issues, the first thing that a martyr brings to a person's mind is fighting on the path of God. Martyrs have taken action, fought, and been martyred in the way of God, Leader underlined.

"A person gives his life for the comfort of others. Someone martyred for security gives his life so that others can live in security. Someone martyred in the Holy Defense gave his life so that the evil, the oppressive enemy could not fulfill the promise he had made to himself about advancing all the way to Tehran and humiliating the Iranian nation," he also pointed out.Imam Khamenei added, "We are in need of the martyrs' messages. We should not assume, 'Well, everyone knows the messages of the martyrs.' No, not everyone knows them. The new generations must be informed about what happened in the past, the motives, their thoughts, and such things. Activities that convey a message have this great benefit."

Imam Khamenei also spoke of how martyrs, martyrdom, and the nations understanding are components that promote national identity. He added that the Iranian nation has achieved greatness in the eyes of the world because of their enthusiasm for martyrdom, "The Iranian nation achieved greatness in the eyes of those who heard about these martyrdoms. Whenever any news leaked out about them, it created greatness for this nation."

The Leader of the Islamic Revolution likened martyrdom to a rosary bead and described it as being the cause of the solidarity that exists between ethnic groups inside the country. He explained this in the following way, "A martyr who was from the north or one who was from the east of the country were all in the same line. They were martyred for a common purpose, for the honor of Islam, for the greatness of the Islamic Republic, and for strengthening Iran. This is what connects these tribes, cities, and regions together. This is the nature of martyrdom."

Referring to the eternal effects and honor of events such as the Shahcheragh tragedy in history, he added, "Each one of the events that has taken place from the time of the Revolution and up until today has remained as a bright spot in history, like a star. The tragedy that took place in the Shahcheragh shrine a few days ago is an eternal star. It will remain in history and be a source of pride and honor. Yes, a number of people were left bereaved. Some of these events are tragic and fill the hearts of human beings with grief, but they are stars. They will remain in history."